My First
500 Words

The Alphabet

Aa

ambulance

Bb

blackboard

Cc

crocodile

Dd

dolphin

Ee

egg

Ff

fairy

Gg

ghost

Hh

helicopter

Ii

ice cream

Jj
jug

Kk
key

Ll
lion

Mm
mountain

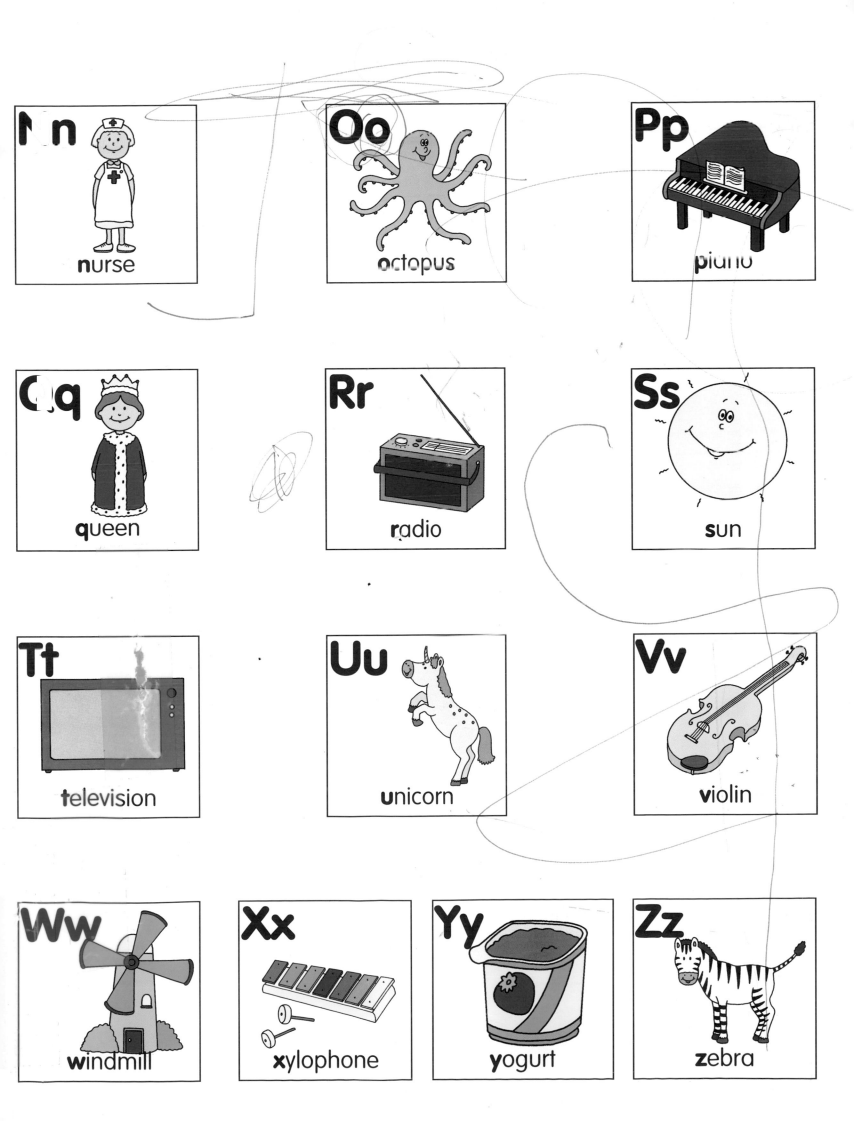

N n nurse

O o octopus

P p piano

Q q queen

R r radio

S s sun

T t television

U u unicorn

V v violin

W w windmill

X x xylophone

Y y yogurt

Z z zebra

Counting to Twenty

1

2

3

4

5

6

7

8

9

10

11

12

13

14

15

16

17

18

19

20

One, two, buckle my shoe,

Three, four, knock at the door,

Five, six, pick up sticks,

Seven, eight, lay them straight,

Nine, ten, a big, fat hen,

Eleven, twelve, dig and delve,

Thirteen, fourteen, maids a courting,

Fifteen, sixteen, maids in the kitchen,

Seventeen, eighteen, maids in waiting,

Nineteen, twenty, my plate's empty.

Shapes

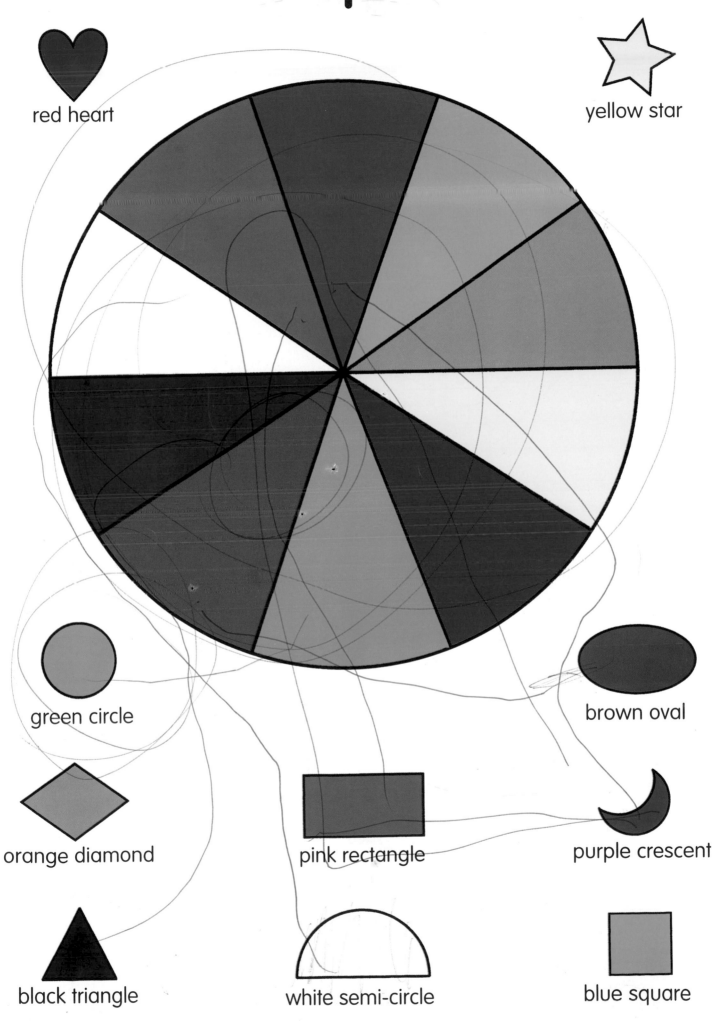

red heart

yellow star

green circle

brown oval

orange diamond

pink rectangle

purple crescent

black triangle

white semi-circle

blue square

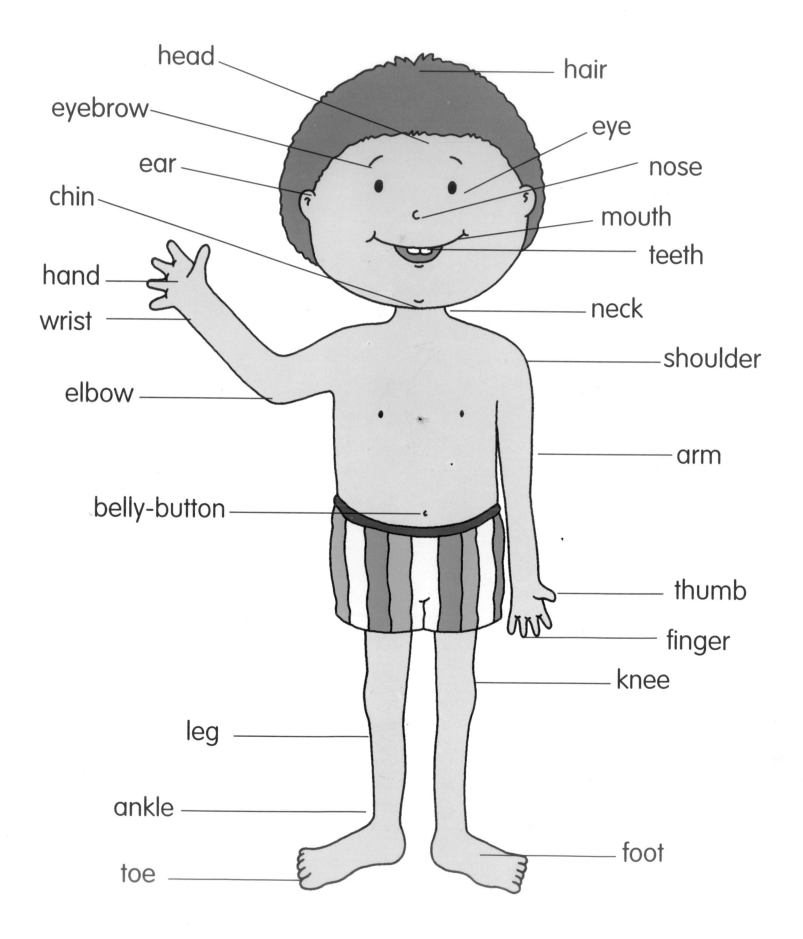

head

hair

eyebrow

eye

ear

nose

chin

mouth

teeth

hand

wrist

neck

shoulder

elbow

arm

belly-button

thumb

finger

knee

leg

ankle

foot

toe

What are they Doing?

climbing

jumping

blowing

swimming

painting

sitting

drawing

skating

standing

sliding

digging

writing

eating

pushing

swinging

washing

drinking

sleeping

Wild Animals

koala

zebra

camel

gorilla

kangaroo

hippopotamus

crocodile

monkey

raccoon

tiger

bear

rhinoceros

lion

elephant

panda

snake

iguana

polar bear

giraffe

beaver

turtle

Pets and Birds

chicken

tortoise

pony

peacock

vulture

hamster

ostrich

dog

rabbit

duck

guinea pig

parrot

goldfish

penguin

swan

mouse

canary

cat

pigeon

Days, Months and Seasons

Monday's child is fair of face.

Tuesday's child is full of grace.

Wednesday's child is full of woe.

Thursday's child has far to go.

Friday's child works hard for a living.

Saturday's child is loving and giving.

But the child that is born on **Sunday**

Is bonny and blithe and good and gay.

January	February	March	April	May	June
July	August	September	October	November	December

In which month is your birthday?

Opposites

a **big** elephant

a **small** mouse

under the bridge

over the bridge

in the box

out of the box

a sunny **day**

a dark **night**

up the stairs

down the stairs

wet raindrops

An umbrella to keep me **dry**

a **fast** rabbit

a **slow** snail

a **happy** face

a **sad** face

hot soup

cold ice cream

a **soft** pillow

a **hard** rock

Time to get Dressed

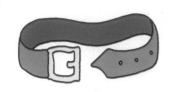
belt

shoes

dress

blouse

socks

hat

skirt   jeans   coat

sweater   t-shirt

scarf

ribbon

zipper

button

shelf

dungarees

jacket

hook

shorts

drawers

hanger

Learn and Play

teacher

picture

scissors

pencils

glue

blackboard

clock

paintbrush

paint

apron

dinosaur

chalk

fingerpaint

desk

crayons

cloth

plant

book

paper

flag

mother

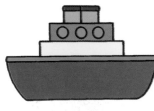

shells

brother

ship

At the Beach

towel

sandcastles

seagull

starfish

beachball

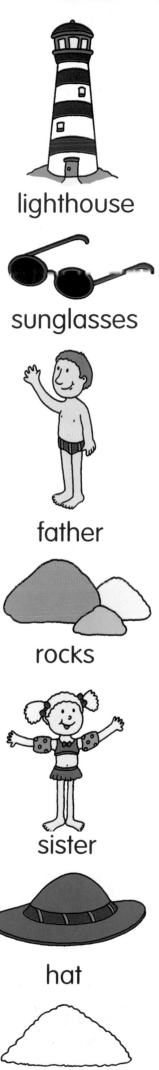

lighthouse

sunglasses

father

rocks

sister

hat

crab   bucket   sea   seaweed   ice cream   sand

Shopping

bread

cucumbers

eggs

cheese

milk

potatoes

grapes

newspaper

oranges

meat

apples

sausages

check-out

pears

basket

purse

money

flowers

bag

carrots

tomatoes

chocolate

bananas

The Doctor's Office

doctor

medicine

spoon

envelopes

watch

thermometer

Band-Aid ™

bandage

cream

nurse

wheelchair

baby

stethoscope

syringe

diary

scissors

calendar

In the Garden

sprinkler

rose

ant

watering can

cabbage

tree

flower pot

lawnmower

grass

cat

leaves

pond

sunflower

nest

bone

rake

bird

dog

bush

wheelbarrow

In the Toy Store

jack-in the-box

doll

teddy bear

train

jigsaw puzzle

plane

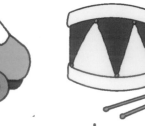

car

drum

computer

blocks

fort

rocking horse

truck

ball

yo-yo

track

clown

trumpet

helicopter

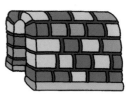

tunnel

A Rainy Day

boots

bridge

fish

umbrella

cloud

frogs

bird

boat

rainbow

blanket

fence

wheel

wall

train

plane

saucepan

puddle

rain hat

rain coat

tent

On the Farm

scarecrow

pig

tractor

goat

cobweb

chicks

duck

horse

lamb

feathers

cow

bucket

stable

turkey

goose

saddle

pig sty

barn

farmer

puppy

pond

Playing in the Snow

ice skates

skis

hat

snowman

mittens

robin

icicles

jacket

pipe

iceberg

coat

scarf

gloves

igloo

mountains

snowflakes

Eskimo

toboggan

snowballs

trees

Working Outside

hammer

drill

toolbox

nails

paint

window

spider

fence

broom

tray

logs

ladder

sack

chimney

garage

car

house

roof

door

By the River

fish

rabbit

bees

tadpole

jar

frog

fishing pole

net

butterfly

squirrel

picnic basket

rock

river

mushroom

beetle

oar

boat

bird

caterpillar

At the Park

kite

fountain

boat

swing

tree-house

see-saw

bench

marbles

buggy

scooter

slide

bicycle

sandbox

rollerskates

skateboard

ball

bat

In the Kitchen

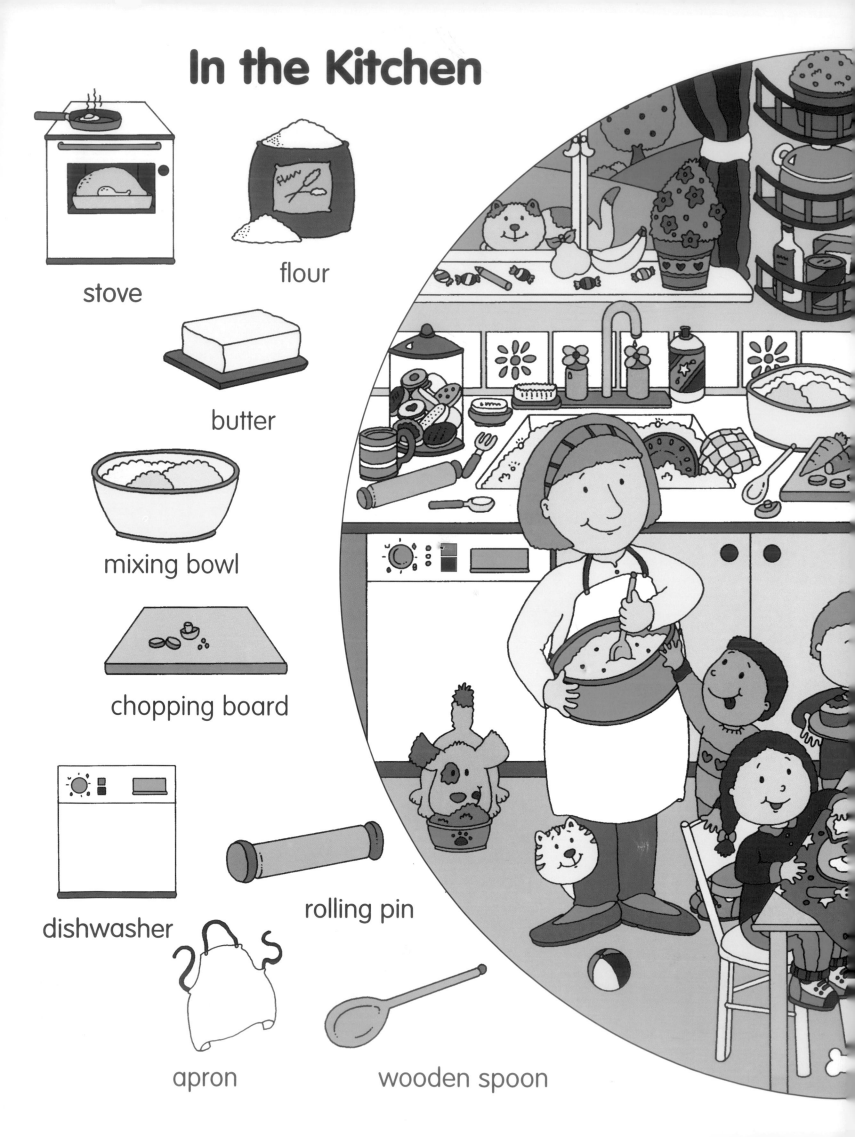

stove

flour

butter

mixing bowl

chopping board

dishwasher

rolling pin

apron

wooden spoon

toaster

microwave

chair

sink

glass

fork

spoon

knife

cup

table

plate

A Birthday Party

cake

sandwiches

balloon

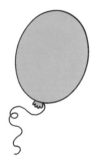
napkin

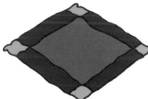
cookie

presents

straw

ice cream

party hat

telephone

milk

necklace

cards

candle

popcorn

tablecloth

camera

pizza

Time for Bed

stars

mirror

brush

comb

bath-tub

soap

sponge

towel

toothbrush

toothpaste

owl

toys

picture

pillow

bed

sheet

lamp

storybook

teddy bear

slippers

rug